I0087060

Copyright © 2016

By Donald MacCoy Williams

This is a work of fiction. Names, characters, businesses, places, events and incidents are either the products of the author's imagination or used in a fictitious manner. Any resemblance to actual persons, living or dead, or actual events is purely coincidental.

Donald MacCoy Williams' Dedications

I would like first & foremost to dedicate this book to my son Elijah. You inspire me to be the best that I can be. Dad-Dad loves you very much lil buddy. Next I would like to dedicate this book to my parents Norman Francis & Gladys Elizabeth Williams. Thanks for bringing me into this world, & for providing me with a foundation. I love you both. This book is also dedicated to my brothers Norman "Bates", Daniel, & (Donnell Artybridge). I love you guys as well.

Donald MacCoy Williams' Acknowledgements

Without Jehovah nothing is possible. Including my voice, words, & the thoughts I use to express myself. So for that I give him my praise & my gratitude. I would like to send a shout-out to Hope Harrison for believing in me & supporting me. I also want to send a shout-out to Fred Miles & Clarence McFadden. I want to send a shout-out to the entire Woodhouse family (Sandra, Earl, Earl Jr., Ronnie & Crystal Alfred) the Sanderson family (Domario, Ricky Sr., Ricky Jr., Barbara, Raleigh Sr., Raleigh Jr., Myra, Pudding, & Troy (RIP), Poppa, Terry, Keisha, Shantel, & Lynette) the Butlers (John Butler Jr., John Butler III aka Lil-Man, Brenda Butler, & Jerome Butler), Mike Alston, Ms. Alston, & Ms. Connie Mills, as well as all of the rest of the Jehovah Witnesses that I grew up with. Though I'll never become one, I appreciate the pleasant company & influences you all provided me with. I want to shout-out all the establishments that I worked @ for putting up with me for as long as they did. I know that I'm a unique & interesting guy to work with, lol. I also want to send a shout-out to Ms. Sharon Wilson, Ms. Linda Kleiber, & the entire staff at Clarence V. Cuffee branch library in Chesapeake, as well as the Horace Downing & the Slover branch libraries in Norfolk, for allowing my children's book "King of the Jungle" to grace their bookshelves. I also want to thank the Slover branch for allowing me to read my children's book @ their branch. I would like to send a major shout-out to The Children's Hospital of The King's Daughter's for allowing me to read my children's book to their patients. Thanks a million. Finally, I want to send a shout-out to Mrs. Adrienne Cromer for helping me bring my poetry book to life. I really appreciate you.

I would like to thank all of my friends and all of my foes. You inspire me.

Reviews for Tears of a Primate

"Tears of a Primate" is a classic.

Daily Bugle

"Tears of a Primate" is a must read. It should be on everyone's bookshelf.

Everythingblack.com

Mr. Williams poetry is simple, yet grabs your attention leaving you thinking.

Hood News

Five Stars!

The Negro Chronicle.

TEARS OF A PRIMATE

BY

DONALD MACCOY WILLIAMS

Affirm the Positive

I am at peace.

I am right where I'm supposed to be.

I am whole just as I am.

I am complete in God's love.

I radiate universal wisdom and love.

The spirit of God is inside me.

God watches over me.

I accept all of my emotions.

I deserve love, serenity and happiness.

Every day I grow wiser, stronger and more loving.

Nothing negative can stand within my way.

I'm Not Your Type.

I figured out why you aren't interested in me.
I'm not your average grade of man, therefore being
with me would cause you to think differently.
My concept of success & life puts me in a category
aside from most men of my ethnicity.
The types of guys that cater to you have no morals or
values, which make them a threat to those within their
communities.
The presence I exude is one of a man who has a plan.
The types of guys that you desire are always in & out
of prison.
I was born with a foundation, which for the most part I
didn't stray too far away from.
The types of guys you're attracted to, if you were to
stand them in front of one of their elders, they would
look real dumb.
For the most part, I can interact with various people
outside my race.
The types of guys that you date, if they tried to hold a
conversation with a foreigner, they would leave the
foreigner with a silly look on his / her face.
I strive to bring honor to my skin as well as my name.

The types of guys that turn you on are proud of
wearing their shame.
The types of guys you lust for have no hope.
The types of guys you want to build a future with
would be better off hanging themselves from a rope.
I hope you can get that "perfect life "that you wish for
so bad.
I also hope that your future husband / baby's daddy
don't do something that will have the both of you
ending up dead.
It's a shame you aren't able to think no further than
your limited intelligence will allow you to.
That's why you're attracted to thugs – they think the
exact way that you do.
They're hard bodies, not God bodies.
Which is why once they've gotten their thrills off of
you, they're going to leave you – useful to nobody.
But if that's what it takes to get you in that comfort
zone.
It's cool, after all no one should be alone.
Just remember though, next time your man slugs you
in the face.
Don't come running up to me, invading my space.
After all, I'm not nor will I ever be.
Your type of man, which is so fortunate for me.

<u>Free</u>

Freedom.

Just what does that word really mean?

We as black people tend to relate that word to the nonexistence of slavery.

Countries or small villages & cities often relate that word to the nonexistence of big countries & governments overthrowing them.

Animals (if they could think), would probably define freedom as the nonexistence of being held in captivity, having the power & ability to roam about within their natural habitats.

Yet what does that word mean to you, & what comes to your mind when that word is mentioned?

We as black people are no longer slaves who get traded off into a lifetime of picking cotton & cooking the master's meals, however we as black people often get hauled off into jail by the cops to spend a lifetime entrapped within steel bars & brick walls.

Small villages & countries are constantly being taken out of exile, yet & still new laws are steadily being made to keep them dependent upon the government that rule them.

So just what is freedom?

To me freedom is a state of mind.

There are thousands of free individuals on this planet;
however they are slaves to their own stupidity.

Which is what usually puts them into a state of captivity.

Freedom is something special.

Freedom is something that is essential to a human's
existence.

Without freedom, a person cease to be an individual-
they become a thing.

Love the fact that you are free.

Cherish the fact that you are free.

And whatever you do, never jeopardize your freedom.

For whoever never appreciated their freedom, they will
soon lose it.

Damaged Goods

I met this cute, thick woman with her hair done up in a
Shirley Temple.
And she said that although her name wasn't Shirley, she
had granted many men access within her temple.
She started pouring out her soul to me- I guess she
assumed that I cared.
And I would've walked away, but in her mental state I
didn't dare.
So I continued to listen to her as she spilled her soul out.
And I could sense she was comfortable in my presence,
because she began telling me of an incident where she
allowed a dozen men to take turns at taking her backseat
out!
Then she began telling me of how she met this drug
dealer who showered her with gifts and fed her a lie of
how he was going to treat her like a queen.
However, on their one night stand, he treated her mean,
and knocked her up and left her at the tender age of 16.
I thought to myself:" That's the age when a girl is
considered to be sweet.
She only keeps company with the elite.
But this woman in front of me spent all her teenage years
being treated like a piece of meat."

Then she kept on about her pregnancy and how her
mental state caused her to have a miscarriage.
And she mentioned that because of the wear and tear on
her body, she was left barren.
The woman looked (physically) intact.
She had a pretty face, a nice rack, and a very sexy back.
Mentally though, this poor woman was gone.
All her life she was mistreated, and left alone.
I wanted to love her, maybe give her a whole new
outlook on life.
After all, I am in the market for a lovely wife.
But she could never be that, for she had been through so
much.
She might get defensive if I raise my voice in an
argument, or I try to extend to her a loving touch.
As we continued there, I soon started thinking about my
own mother.
"Was her life somewhat like this before she met my
father, and had me and my two brothers?"
Treat every woman that you come into contact with the
utmost amount of respect.
And parents, be an active part of your children's lives-
never show them neglect.

Teach our children of the future to be strong role models
within their neighborhoods.
Or they will end up like this woman- just another case of
damaged goods.

<u>Led Astray</u>

Once I knew of a kid from around my way.

He was raised right, but his knucklehead friends led him astray.

He was a copycat- monkey see, monkeys gotta do.

He was a follower, so if the majority did it, then he would do it too.

The first few years of his cutting up proved to turn out in his favor.

Just like his idiot friends, he too would cause trouble for his neighbors.

If a buddy of his made a move, all you had to do was give him the word.

Next thing you saw was him grabbing old ladies purses, running off & all the while flipping them back the bird.

His take from stealing those purses grew & grew.

Which is why he was always getting hit-up for money from those same hoodlums he knew.

He couldn't tell them no, after all they were his friends.

He wanted to be accepted, so when asked he always gave up his ends.

He continued to do this until his funds were depleted.

And since he was a sucker, all he could do was go broke & stay heated.

Finally one day, he felt as if he had tolerated enough.

He got him & his unsavory friends together to go & rob
Hampton Roads Federal Savings & Trust.

In the process of the robbery, a bank teller & a guard got
popped.

And he would've gotten away with it, except his so-
called friends snitched him out to the cops.

Now his life flashed before his very eyes, when the judge
& jury pronounced him guilty.

And the sentence for his crime was the death penalty.

His choices in life wasn't very nice.

He was a wild boy, so for his last meal he had wild game
with a side order of wild rice.

If only he had become his own man, & didn't follow
people.

Then the state wouldn't be injecting his arm with that
needle.

Last words he said before he burst puss like a zit.

He quoted 1 Corinthians 15:33 which reads: Bad
association spoils useful habits.

Me … With Pride

When my name protrudes from a person's lips, especially
from those of a close friend, relative, relative, or lover, I
expect it to be said with pride- say my name.
When a person is in my company, especially my mate, I
expect her head to be held high with a radiant smile
looking her very best- be with me.
When a person has a possession of mine that I trust, I
expect them to treat the merchandise as if it was theirs-
use it in good faith. (What's mine is yours).
When a person thinks of me, I can only hope that they
have pleasant thoughts of me, & that I am in their
prayers- think of me- pray for me.

That Goodness

I want that thing from you - it's deep & it's wet.
And rumor has it that if I tried to put it in my mouth, it
would tempt my palate.
Right now, I won't go that far cause we haven't known
each other long enough.
I have to get acquainted with you before I even Think
about doing that stuff.
But I know you still want to tease me with it.
Tender, don't you want me to be pleased with it?
We can cuddle if you want, but only for a bit.
Cause that thing on you is very desirable, & I want to
pound it.
I want to be up in it long enough to explore.
Allow me to study your walls & all, while I have you
begging for more.
If I stay down there too long, you might shoot out a
milky substance.
No need for me to be alarmed, that's just to let me know
that you're loving it.
Not many men can cause you to erupt, or so I was told.
A mutual friend of ours mentioned that you haven't
gushed since you were 21 yrs. old.

Even though this will be my first time with you, it
certainly won't be my last.

After we get done, I'm going to always have access to
that ass.

Most men get what they want, regardless if the woman
gets off or not.

They don't try to even search for a woman's spot.

However, I know where yours' is, so I'm going to strike
it every time.

And our spots are located in the same area- that's in our
minds.

The Sweetest Mother of All

I'm not ashamed to say that I have the sweetest mother
over everyone.
She may not be the smartest woman in the world,
however what smarts that she does possess she uses them
to provide the best she can for me.
My mother may not be the prettiest woman of all,
however her looks eventually landed her a good man who
actually cares for/about her as well as myself.
My mother may not be the richest woman that I know,
however the money that she does make, she spends
wisely so we can eat and have a roof over our heads.
My mother may not have the newest vehicle that's out,
however the car she does have gets us back and forth to
where we need to be (consistently).
My mother may not be the best cook when she's in the
kitchen, however when she cooks, she makes sure that I
eat healthy.
My mother may not be the strongest woman in the world,
however you better not mess with her.
She will kick your butt!!
There are a lot of things that my mother will never be nor
will she ever have.

But she will still be the sweetest mother in the world. Simply because she's my mother and I know she loves me with all of her heart.

Black Power

I'm a positive black man but, don't be fooled.

If things get thick I'm reaching for my tool.

These damn Caucasians want to commit genocide upon my race. To get us

To get us erased they will try and shoot us all in the face.

In South Carolina, a young white man preyed upon an all black church.

Everyday right there he perched and he lurked.

Waiting for the opportune time to kill God's children.

The white man even prayed with the black people inside of God's building.

Next what he did was down-right low.

He walked out to his car, popped the trunk, grabbed his rifle came back in the church, and let that thang go.

What's worse is that this sick fuck is going to get off in court.

His lawyer will say he was off his meds that day and his brain hurt.

Couldn't have been me in that church with Mr. Dylan Roof.

Tears Of A Primate

A nigger like me will beat his ass, take him up to the top
of a church, slit his throat, then leave
him dying on the roof.

Too many children of my race are being killed off, & it
has got to stop.

This message goes out to all Klansman, gang-bangers,
old-fashioned bigots, & cops.

The black man is the original human to wander this
Earth.

If you don't believe me, do your research, & see the facts
for what they're worth.

My skin is my beauty.

My black is what defines me.

I could never be a sell-out, because I'll always have my
complexion to remind me,

That I come from nothing.

And that people will write me off as nothing.

However, through God's will & my drive, I'm going to
accomplish something.

There's more to us black people than what we're given
credit for.

In this country, that's what the Willie Lynch system was
put in place for.

Tears Of A Primate

An unconscious Negro stops his fellow Negro from rising.

And that's a joy to the Caucasians when they see us not monopolizing & enterprising.

As a people we have to learn that there's strength in numbers.

If & when we decide to stick together, our days of living on this Earth become brighter.

And all of us are faced with the same issues & concerns, whether our shade is darker or lighter.

Racism affects all races.

Not just one by itself.

Each race depends on another race to help its prosperity & wealth.

If one of us go, we all die.

Don't be fooled by the white man's evil tactics & his lies.

That's how our black asses stay down, while these other races rise.

The only race with no unity amongst them is us.

We're also the race that no other races trust.

Wake up my brothers & sisters.

It's time we stop being ignorant, & we stand up for ourselves.

Let's stop pumping money into Amerikkka's economy,
& start building a stream of wealth for ourselves.

Let's educate our children & get them out of these public
schools.

With these European's public school system, they're
going to have our children graduating as damn fools.

And if you think this is all a coincidence, you're crazy.

This is all in an attempt to portray us Negroes as being
troublesome & lazy.

Which is the perfect excuse to use come time for them to
annihilate us all.

It's up to each and every black person to prevent his/ her
own downfall.

We're in our last days of the Apocalypse, therefore, ain't
much time to waste.

Become conscious, & understand your origin before it's
too late.

Each one, teach one.

Create a place within your mental space.

One hand washes the other.

And both hands watch the face.

Church

Ahhh, church.

That luxurious building with that tall, beautiful steeple.

On Sundays, you can count on it being filled with lots of people.

There is at least 2 or 3 in every community.

For the life of me I don't know why.

All I see is well-dressed individuals going in & out of them as I drive by.

The parking lots of these churches is packed with nice whips.

None of them are dented, rusted, or have paint that's chipped.

If you need a ride to any one of these churches, most of them have vans that will pick you up.

And you won't be charged for gas, so as long as once you get there, you put some $ in their cup.

If you don't put $ in the church's cup, the pastor or the bishop has a way of carrying you.

They will get on the platform, give a sermon, & during that sermon, they will talk about you.

Once you get offended or embarrassed enough, you're going to do either one of two things.

Either you're going to run out of the church & never come back, or you're going to cough up some $ or come off your expensive necklaces/ rings.

The members of the churches are profiting off the lost souls of those who know no better.

They mislead their flocks into thinking that if they come to church every Sunday & make their pastors, reverends, & bishops rich, their lives will become better.

True, some of the churches have food banks, & that's all cool & dandy.

But please, if you're going to feed your communities, give them more than just outdated foods & pieces of candy.

People need the word of God which provides faith & hope for a brighter tomorrow. When people see God cares for them & their situations, that assurance erases people's sorrows.

People with positions in churches should be striving to change the hearts & minds of our youth.

And the best way to start that process is by telling them the truth.

Pastors, quit telling people to pray for success & wealth.

Instead, encourage your congregation to promote love of thou fellowman & good health.

Stop making people think that God & his son Jesus were white.

Quit making people that they're going to hell if they don't do right.

Exodus 33:20 states that "you cannot see my face, for no one may see me and live."

Therefore, how can all these pastors & preachers have these detailed images of God & his home, & yet live?

Church is big business. No more. No less. And pastors/ preachers are simply motivational speakers who encourage you to pay them, if you expect to be blessed.

If you want to be close with God, simply go to him in prayer.

Just tell God you want to live in his love, & he will guide you there.

Man can't lead another man to God's favor.

It's silly to think a sinner can guide you to a more supreme & perfect being.

Use your own intelligence to find out God's purpose for you.

Upon another person's intelligence & life experience's you shouldn't be leaning.

Save your money or give it to a homeless person in need.

They could use that money more, & that's an even more noble deed.

Than handing it over to a man whose mind is full of deceit, & whose heart is filled with greed.

On Sundays spend time praising God without gathering in a big building.

You can honor God just by being in the house with your family, chilling.

God will recognize your worship the same as if you did it in a church.

All in all, YOU yourself get right with God.

Not you get right with God via a prestigious pastor & his mega-church.

I Don't Know

I never knew what it was to be disenfranchised.

However, I do know about hard times.

I don't know nothing about slinging packs or committing violent crimes.

I do know the concept of trying to make a dollar out of a dime.

I don't know anything about being raised solely by my mother.

I do however, have two parents who settled for less, and used Jehovah God and their religious beliefs as a cover.

I don't know anything about living in the ghetto.

I do know about growing up in the projects.

I guess that's why like so many African Americans, I too like nice material objects.

I don't know anything about the white man holding me back.

I do know about being suppressed.

I also know about putting on a great performance under duress.

I don't know who the greatest rapper is, and I really don't care.

Because in my eyes, whoever it is, KRS-ONE or Rakim helped to pave the way for him or her to be there.

I don't know how to lick off a shot.

I do know how to bang.

And you do too.

Simply hook-up with your significant other, and you two do yall's thang.

I don't know a lot of Ebonics.

I do know the latest lingo.

I've never hit it big in a casino.

However, one time I did win a lot of money playing bingo.

I don't know anything about a ménage a trios'.

I do know about sexcapades.

I don't want to throw lavish parties.

However, I do want to enjoy myself in the cascades.

What I'm trying to convey is that I too have the same trials and tribulations as most of yall.

Only thing, is I think differently than most of yall.

And if you think I'm being pompous or arrogant, for the sake of not arguing, I'll say I guess so.

However, to be honest with you, I really don't know.

Tears Of A Primate

The Luv I Never Knew

I think I'm in luv y'all.

I say it's luv because the feeling I have inside of me for this woman is strong.

And the only two strong feelings I've ever had for someone was luv or hate.

And it damn sure ain't hate.

The feeling I have for this woman is keeping me up all night.

The feeling I have for this woman has me off focus when I'm at work.

The feeling I have for this woman allows me not to be scared of things that normally would frighten me.

Only luv can do that. I mean this woman don't know how bad this feeling is that's going on within me.

The feeling I have for this woman will give me the ability to defend her & protect her from any type of harm that comes her way.

The feeling that I have for this woman makes me want to go out & make all the money in the world so I can give her the world.

The feeling that I have for this woman has no bounds.

There's no limit as to what I'll do or become for this woman because this feeling of luv that I have for her has taken over me.

Or is it luv?

Could it be lust?

Only time will tell.

Trapped

I done fucked up y'all.

Yesterday I received an email from a female I slept with.

In the email, she stated that I got her pregnant.

I don't want to believe any of this, nor do I want that child to be mine's.

But me being the idiot that I am, the child is more than likely mine's.

I didn't love this female, so why did I have unprotected sex with her?

Better yet, why did I have sex with her period?

I was brought up in a Christian home, & my parents taught me about abstaining from having premarital sex with females I had no intentions on marrying.

But no, I couldn't listen.

So I started having sexual intercourse with just about every female that wanted to sleep with me.

I guess by me sleeping with multiple women that gave me a false sense of self-worth.

I used to brag about how I had slept with a lot of women, & yet I didn't get any STD's from them, nor did I get any of them pregnant.

In my head, I thought that I was sterile.

Ain't no way a man can sleep with as many females as I did & not get them pregnant, unless he was shooting blanks I used to tell myself.

So with that false & inaccurate sense of security, I continued sleeping with various females & not using any type of protection.

The bull-shit that I was on stayed great for a long time, so I had no intentions on stopping the dangerous & ignorant deed that I was doing.

I was pounding them down, just giving these females that sexual pleasure they so desired.

In return, some of them gave me various things of value.

Some bought me gifts such as clothes, a down payment on a car, some $ to pay a few fines & a few small bills with.

A couple of females even gave me some spending $.

I felt like "The Man" at that point.

Nobody could tell me my dick wasn't made of gold.

Then one day I met this female.

Little did I know she was going to change my life in a major way.

I thought of her as a cool female, so I hung out with her, & that went on for a few weeks.

That's when I decided to have casual sex with her.

"After all, that's what I had been having with these other females, & didn't anything bad come of it, so why would things change now": I thought to myself.

Only problem was this female was looking to have another child to go with the one she already had.

And she didn't care who the guy was, or if the guy was going to marry, or be in a relationship with her.

Just as long as she got her bundle of joy.

I beat the pussy up & smiled from ear to ear while I was doing it.

She was thinking that I was going to be the sucker to give her a child, & she was smiling from ear to ear while she let me have my way with her.

We did the deed, & we went our separate ways.

I lost contact with her, & went on about my life.

A year & some months later, I received a subpoena at my place stating that I need to come to the court in order to take a paternity test.

It seems the female had a child since the last time me & her slept together.

I'm in shock & bewilderment at this point, however an order from the court is an order from the court, & I'm not about to be arrested for failure to appear in court.

So I go to court, & I let them do what they have to do in order to determine if I'm a father or not.

The results come back.

And low & behold, I AM A FATHER!!

That's when I start bursting into tears.

"How am I going to take care of this child?"

"I don't make enough money to take care of myself & a child!"

"I can't be late with my child support payments, otherwise I'm going to jail, & I can't afford that!"

All those thoughts, plus many more came to my mind once the reality hit that I was a father.

"I'm in for it now.": I kept thinking to myself.

All of this time I was having unprotected sex with all of these females, God was watching over me, because he knew just as well as I did that I wasn't ready to take on being a parent.

So in spite of my stupidity, God allowed me to walk away safe from my sexual encounters - clean & free.

However, after a while, God became tired & frustrated with me doing the same ignorant misdeeds over & over again.

That's when he had to teach me a hard lesson.

And the lesson God had to teach me was that you can't keep ignoring him & expect not to suffer in the end.

Now I'm stuck as a parent to a child that I love – by a female I don't love ☹.

Your Average Guy

There's more to me than me being a lover.

There's more to me than me making a woman my baby's mother.

There's more to me than me being a close friend.

There's more to me than me trying to represent all men.

There's more to me than me being a jerk.

There's more to me than me being an individual who just works.

There's more to me than me being another man's son.

There's more to me than me just wanting to have fun.

There's more to me than me being a man who will instantly transform his life to find favor with God.

There's more to me than me portraying the life of someone who's had it hard.

There's more to me than wanting to be a poster boy.

There's more to me than me being someone's play-toy.

There's more to me than me being a musician.

I want to do something other than run my mouth while people listen.

There's more to me than being a person that takes charge.

There's more to me than me being a person that wants to
live large.

If I had to sum it all up…what I would like to say is,

I just want to be your average everyday…kind of guy.

I'll Trade in My Life for a Good Night's Sleep

Oh what I wouldn't do for a peaceful night's rest.

Just the *idea* of me enjoying a long decent nap makes me tired.

No worries, no cares.

All there is for me to consider is how I want to lay on the bed.

(And even then that won't be a real thought…
my body will find a comfortable position sooner or later).

Scientific studies show that the average human needs 7 to 8 hours of sleep to function properly.

I'd be lucky if I got 4 hours of sleep.

Within my atmosphere, all that I'm around is loud noise.

Kids playing and crying and the television blaring at its highest level.

God, how I wish it would go away while I'm sleeping!

My dreams would be fascinating.

Then when I rose out of bed, I'd be well-rested and ready to take charge of my day.

Forgive me, if I seem frustrated, it's only because I am.

I haven't slept well in months and my body is wearing down.

My attitude is changing as well.

Normally I'm low-key, gentle and mild-mannered.

However, lately I've been loud, grouchy and obnoxious.

I'm getting restless.

But the way things seem, the next time I see a good
night's rest is when I take my

dirt nap.

In All These Years

In all these years of my life, never really took anytime to ponder about anything-

especially what lies ahead for me.

So, now as I'm thinking, it's difficult for me to determine as to what path I want to

take.

So on to something else a little less complicating.

Next, I focus my thoughts on who the ideal woman for me is.

I've never really had any intimate relationship; therefore, in all my years of living,

I can't base certain qualities of a woman as being good or bad.

So that's the end of that.

Then I start to concentrate on other things that normally I wouldn't care about.

The more I tried to put those thoughts and questions out of my mind,

the stronger the affect they had on my thinking ability.

Pretty soon, I totally freaked out!

What's causing all of this?

Could I have finally gained a conscience after all of these years?

Or is my level of maturity and understanding finally catching up to me?

That's just too much for me to come to terms with!

For the first time in all of my life I actually took time to examine the important things needed in my life!

Before long, that incident was over and to this day,

I'm happy to say that that hasn't happened again!

<u>Letter to My Ex</u>

Word around town is you've got a new nigga and you two are happy.

But if that shit is true, then why is your friend saying you want to come back to

me?

Could it be that they're causing drama by stating things that's false?

Or is it true you want to be reunited back with me so you can get your salad tossed?

I will have to admit it was fun when I was fucking with your ass.

But one thing I don't believe in is going back to my past.

I'm in a relationship also with someone new, and I'll be damned if I fuck that up for a cheap screw.

You left me 'cause you said you wanted a change, and now you want me to drop my girl for you- Bitch you must be insane!

The sex we have be off the hook and don't even talk about the way that she looks!

She has street smarts and other vast amounts of knowledge; however, you're dumb as shit and you spent 4 years in college!

What nerve you have coming to me as if nothing's changed!

I can't think of all the damage you've done to my brain with all your games.

Grow up---take control of your life!

Maybe you might luck up and become someone else's wife.

Ex means no longer and we're no longer together.

Now leave me alone and get your shit together!

When the Fire Dies

Love is like a spark of fire.

One burns through obstacles, the other burns with desire.

Over a period of time, the flame can become stronger and stronger.

It can cover miles, maybe even longer.

To make the flame more powerful, you have to constantly feed it, and the minute you fail to do so and the fire dies,

Fire when controlled is something so simply fascinating, when uncontrolled, it's very dangerous and breathtaking.

The damage from a fire can be priceless, and can leave your bank account not looking its nicest.

Fire is a mixture of colors.

Love is colorblind and can match up to any color.

Whatever size your fire is, continue to keep it burning, and if you have a soul mate, do your utmost to keep that person yearning.

Keep your love away from temptation.

Keep your fire away from water.

Watch out for your actions and those of others.

Keep the fire alive and rising.

I am Death

My name is Death.

I can take on various forms and I can reach your anywhere.

You can't escape me; all you can do is face me.

And with that in mind, I sometimes ask myself: "Why aren't people afraid of me?"

Don't people realize that at any point and time I could come for them

and take them off into an eternity of nonexistence?

When I go out on my daily round, all I see is people moving about,

doing whatever it is that makes their hearts content,

not even at once acknowledging my existence.

Could it be that within the last few years a majority of mankind

has turned to God to give them the faith and strength that they need to face me?

I've also noticed that a few individuals like to take drugs

in order to ease the pain of confronting me.

However, that doesn't concern me none.

I'll take whoever I can in whatever condition I can take them in.

So ask yourself:

"Are you happy with your live and all your accomplishments so far?"

If not, do what you have to in order to rectify that predicament, because when I come for you,

I'll be coming full blast....

And there's nothing you can do to stop me.

Finding Myself

Pardon me, but have you seen a guy with a pair of black jeans and a black T-shirt?

I think that he might be disturbed or seriously hurt.

Never have I seen a person in that sad of a state.

My guess is that he's consumed with a lot of revenge and hate.

I really need to find this guy, so help me please...

Even if not for him, do it to put <u>my</u> soul at ease.

Last I heard he was traveling north...back to the place of his birth.

Knowing him he probably has no I.D. or any cash.

So therefore he probably doesn't have a real place to stash.

He has no friends, but he has dozens of foes,

and most of them are either free-loading niggas or no ass good hoes.

Man, why I let him walk out on me the way that he did?

All I did was scream at him and told him he acted like a kid.

I didn't mean to break his heart-

If anything happens to him; however, minds will be shattered all apart.

Oops, I almost forgot! He also like to make people laugh a lot.

Tears Of A Primate

So if you see a crowd of people laughing, that means
where hot on his trail…

and then eventually we'll catch up to his tail.

OOO…what he can't imagine the trouble he's in,

fortunate for him he is my best friend.

Sir, you've got to help me find him- I'll even give you all
of my wealth.

I'm willing to give you anything-just help me find my
inner-self!

When I Die

When I die I wonder how it will be.

Will there be a large amount of people paying their respects to me?

Will there be lots of moaning and weeping; or will a majority of the attendants end up sleeping?

How will my parents and brothers handle the situation?

Will there be lots of comforting?

Or will everyone start fault-finding and hating?

I was taught about Jehovah and the resurrection hope.

So I guess me knowing that enables me to cope.

How will my life be taken from me?

Will I die from a disease or will it all happen accidentally?

There's lots of enemies I've made in my life…

So maybe I might get gunned down or perhaps even knifed.

However, all of this is just the half of what I want to know.

When I die, I would also like to know where I'm gonna' go.

Will I go to heaven or will I go to hell?

Whichever one I go to, will I be received in well?

What colors will I wear? Red, black or white?

Tears Of A Primate

Will my corpse be heavy or will it be light?
Another thing- based on where I go, what jobs must I
perform? And my body temperature- will it be below
zero degrees or will it be warm?
Wherever I go, will I be allowed to have sex….
or must I watch other people until I become vexed?
And what's this reincarnation thing all about?
Though I may sound very anxious and curious…
I'm in no real hurry to find out.

Love

Love is many a splendored thing or so I was taught.

Love is also something that cannot be bought.

Some even say love is blind...and when discovered by

the wrong person... it can drive that individual out of

his/her mind.

Love can cause you to go out of your way,

just to ensure yourself that you've made someone else's

day (even if you have a miserable one).

Love has even been said to know no bounds.

If you go on a timeless journey, if a person is close to

you,

love will make that person wait around.

Seems as if love is stupid to me;

seems as if cupid doesn't have a clue to me.

Because if something is blind and it knows no limits,

it seems as if eventually it will land into a pit.

Maybe that explains why one man will try and take

another man's life; if he catches that man sleeping with

his wife.

Or maybe that's why a woman will tolerate a man

punching her in her face.

Instead of taking some kind of action and getting out of

that place. Guess I'll never know what love means (not

that I really want to)

unless it comes to me in the form of a dream.

So all in all if you have sense,

you'll hopefully realize love makes absolutely no sense!

The Woman of My Desire

The woman of my desire, oh where can she be?

Where is that woman that's just right for me?

Is she under a rock? Is she in a library?

Is she in a vineyard picking berries?

Or is she already in a relationship she can't get out of?

Does she know there's someone else in the world to love?

Is she fat or is she skinny?

Does she have one or two dependents or does she have many?

Does she have a positive attitude about herself and life?

Tell me where-oh-where is my future wife?

Though I sound desperate, I'm really not…

I just don't want my high hopes to get shot.

So until I find her or until she finds me…

I'll preoccupy myself being lonely.

My Wife

Today I was bored, with nothing to do…

So to preoccupy myself, I decided to list the reasons as to why I love you.

I love you because you're so laidback…

I love you because you look so splendid in tight slacks.

I love you because whenever I go out, you don't worry

as to when I'll be back…

I love you because you put up with so much of my crap.

I love you because of who you are…

I love you for the fact that you trusted me

not to flirt with other women when I was working at the bar.

I love you because of your radiant smile,

I love you because whenever I need you, I know you'll go that extra mile.

I love you because you come from a decent family…

And I love the fact that they try to get along with me.

I love you because you're a woman that's willing to compromise…

I love you because whenever I need advice, you can give me answers that's sometimes wise.

I love you because if there's something you really want, you're willing to make a sacrifice.

No wonder I chased you to be my wife!

(And I'm damn proud that I did!)

Sooner or Later

Sooner or later, you're gonna' get yours.

You're too ignorant to change that.

It's sad how you dodge reality instead of facing the facts.

Sooner or later, you'll sit back and reminisce;

As to how many real friends on your list that you mistreated and dissed.

Then you might hear of one on their way to fame…

And at an awards ceremony in their honor, they forget to mention your name.

Can't blame that person, because you had that coming to you all along…

Stupid fool, how long can you let this continue on?

Stabbed your right hand man in the back, for a fellow that didn't respect you.

The guy didn't give you anything out of the funds he had due.

Fucking foolish bastard, you're going to pay for selling me out!

And I guarantee it's gonna' be sooner or later- No Doubt!!!

<u>Why not Dress Clothes?</u>

Seems like niggas don't wanna' dress casual no more.

Everywhere I shop, I'll see a suit in a store.

Waiting for someone to take it home,

Why-oh-why don't guys want to put suits on?

Could it be they think they'll look like fools?

Or perhaps maybe, it takes away from their being cool.

Personally, I'm not concerned with either one,

because either in jeans or dress slacks, I get the job done.

Hell, some of your most notorious gangsters wore suits;

Which probably explains how they always got away with the loot.

True, suits can be hot at times…

That's why I never wear a suit coat and time with mine.

Still it gives me the results as if I did-

It's just that I'm sick of looking like a damn kid!

If you look like you're young in the head…

You'll probably attract someone whose brain is completely dead.

However, if you throw a dress outfit on…

You might attract someone who is beautiful, kind and warm.

So next time you see someone in a suit-

Don't just think they're trying to be cute.

In actuality they could be rowdy…and definitely *bout it-bout it*!

White Death

Hi, my name is Crack- and I say that quite sadly;

Because unlike *butt crack*, I'm very deadly.

Fucking with me, you can lose your house and home…

Fucking with me, can make you all alone.

One sniff or taste of me can have you wanting more;

I can turn a well-respected woman into a whore.

Man, shit I even got pimps beat;

I'm the primary reason women even walk the streets.

Getting dicked for some cash, then take that loot and buy pound of my white ass.

Sadly, they go right out again; however, this time they go fuck over their friends.

All for the love of my white skin.

You don't believe me?

Well, here take this spoon….

Now cook me and smoke me- see if I don't have you howling at the moon.

I warn you, don't lose your top.

Because I'm like Orville Redenbacher-

Tears Of A Primate

Once you pop, you ain't gonna' stop.

Although I look pretty, I'm nothing nice…

Trying to mix company with me, you'll pay the ultimate price.

Gangsta'

I am a gangster. I cause chaos for a living.

Why? I don't know. Why? I don't really care.

Some people say it's due to me having a one-parent
family-

Some even say it's due to the lack of respect for myself.

But they just don't know me.

Lots of people sit around on their asses pointing and
complaining that people

don't have enough goal, yet nobody wants to help and
individual to find some.

So I'm helping myself.

Hopefully, I'll get that job at I.B.M. that I tried out for
last year.

Then after that, I'm gonna' get my three kids and their
mother into a three story condominium.

By that time I'll be ready to put some money into a bank

so my kids can have some college tuition.

Matter of a fact, while we're talking about it, I'm going
to buy me a suit and get a haircut

so I'll be ready for my next interview-

just as soon as I rob you for your keys and your wallet.

<u>Why</u>

"Why are things going downhill around me?"- I
sometimes ask myself.

I want to pretend that I don't know so I'll block the real
answer out of my mind

and come up with questions to derail myself such as:

Why do people try so hard to get material possessions,
yet when they finally get them they can't enjoy them
because they have to continue to struggle just to keep
them?

Or why is it that a father will join the military to learn
discipline, bravery and honor, fight a war against a
country of total strangers and die for his country, yet will
avoid a family he created?

Why will a woman give her body to a man who has no
genuine love or respect for her
when there's a man out there who can give that and
more?

Why is it that an upcoming star from the projects will
stay in the projects just to prove that he's a real
individual?

Why do policemen swear on an oath to protect and serve,
yet you see them harassing and whipping on the
innocent, while the criminals are allowed to continue in
their wrongdoing?

Why does the government spend millions of dollars on
weapons, yet closes its eyes on the homeless and hungry?

Hell, why do young people disrespect older people?

Finally, I had no choice but to come to the realization that

the reason the world is in such a chaos is Adam, Eve and Satan.

They spread sin and imperfection amongst all of us.

I Cry

I cry because I'm very depressed.

I also cry because I'm so stressed.

I cry because I feel so used.

I cry because I've been mentally abused.

I should be ashamed to cry, but I'm not.

After all it's not like I cry a lot.

I cry because I see bad things that I cannot change.

I cry so I can release my inner pains.

I cry due to lack of self-esteem,

sometimes I don't even consider myself to be a human being.

I cry as a way of showing sympathy,

regret, fear and empathy.

I cry because I'm out of answers.

I cry because I just found out that I got cancer.

I cry because I'm running out of time

and tears are a form of easing my mind.

I cry because there's nothing to do,

I cry because I can't be with you.

I cry for I'm becoming deranged,

I cry so I can watch the color of my eyes change.

I cry when I'm cutting onions up,

I cry when I've received a stroke of good luck.

I'll for any reason known to man.

After all, I cry merely because I can.

Bill Clinton

When I think of Bill Clinton

These words come to mind...

Devoted father, husband...

Pervert.

Political leader pet owner...

Lewinsky.

Jazz musician, peace negotiator...

Player.

White man, president...

Sugar daddy.

College graduate, frat brother...

Cradle robber.

And finally, celebrity, a part of history...

Chester the molester.

<u>Stunt Dummy</u>

Hi my name is Bob Clemmons and I'm a stuntman.

My job is dangerous, yet it's fun.

You see, my job is to do the stunts that the actors prefer not to do on their movies.

For instance, yesterday an actor had to drive a car from one rooftop

and jump over to another one.

He wasn't sure that he would be able to make the jump, so he had me to fill in for him.

Well, I damn near killed myself doing the jump; however, I made it successfully!

And today, there's a stuntman needed for a scene where an actor goes

through a cage of about ten lions with a stun gun.

Nobody want to seem to take the stunt, so I guess that's another calling for me to risk my life.

You're right---I know it sounds stupid, but somebody has to do it.

Besides, it pays the bills.

Well, if I'm going to take the stunt I'm going to have to sign the fill-in board,

so I have to get going.

But before I go, I'd like to say two things:

Tears Of A Primate

In order to be a stuntman,

you have to be very agile and you have to have no fears.

So goodbye and wish me luck.

See ya'!

King of the Jungle

Once upon a time there was a lion by the name of Leo. He was appointed the king of the entire jungle.

"What an honor": thought Leo to himself.

So off he went to tell the other animals the news.

"I am king of the jungle. Whatever I say do, you have to do it-- or leave":

proclaimed Leo to the giraffes.

Angered by this, the giraffes left the jungle.

Next, Leo approached the parrots. "I am king of the jungle.

Whatever I say do, you have to do it-- or leave": he again bragged.

Also angered by Leo's statement, the parrots left the jungle.

Eventually, Leo made sure that all the animals of the jungle knew that he was indeed the king.

And just like the giraffes and the parrots, all of the animals became angry and left.

That is all except the tigers.

Being that tigers and lions are of the same species,

they were sympathetic and understanding towards Leo's attitude

—up until he made the tiger aware of his prominent position.

Then they too left.

Now being that there were no more animals left to rule,

Leo was no longer king of the jungle and,

he too eventually ended up leaving the jungle.

After all, how can you rule over subjects you no longer have?

Music

Sounds are everywhere around you. Even when you don't want them to be.

Some sounds are irritating while other affect you pleasantly.

Birds chirping, rain falling and even water streaming.

There are even sounds that you hear while you're dreaming.

However, I like sounds that follow a certain beat.

Especially the ones that cause me to dance in the streets.

And I love soft music playing in the background...

When me and that special lady is about to throw down.

Even when I'm going to work, I enjoy a soft melody-

That way while I'm working, there will be a rhythm within me.

Music affects everyone to say the least...

After all, music calms the savage beast.

The Hunt is On

I am hungry. I haven't eaten a bite in hours.

So I dig through some nearby rubble in search of food.

Suddenly, I see a herd of playful gazelles!

Wow how my stomach and mouth long for one of them!

That's when everything before me focuses on one goal…

GET THE GAZELLE!

First…Seek out the weakest one. Then…Hunt it down.

The reward….Eat it up!

So next, I let out a blood-curdling roar to let them know that I'm in their midst.

They become afraid and start running for their precious lives.

All of them are pretty fast-that is, all except for you.

You're the smallest, the weakest and the most scared.

Ahhh… the ideal prey!!

I don't want to eat you right away- (I like to play with my food).

So I let you get a running head start.

You look so desirable- the way you run…your delicious scent and your plump, juicy body.

Damn, I go to have you!! I can't wait any longer.

Now I must give chase.

Eventually, I catch up to you.

You put up a good fight but still, you're no match for me.

After a few blows from my claws, I knock you down and out for the count.

Now I close in for the kill.

Just like I thought…you taste so delicious!!

I'm finished with your remaining carcass; however, later on I will get hungry again…

That's when I'll hunt down one of your relatives!

Priorities

I told myself one day that I needed to get my priorities straight.

The first thing I told myself I was going to do was to get

a decent education so I could get a decent job.

The second thing I told myself I was going to do was to get

a decent bank account so I could get a decent home.

The third thing I told myself I was going to do was to get

a decent means of transportation.

Eventually, those things fell into place as I wanted.

Yet I wasn't satisfied.

"What could be missing?" I thought to myself.

Finally I figured it out.

I should've told myself that I was going to get a decent relationship with God

so that I could become a decent person and perhaps find myself a decent mate and friend.

Like a Gun

A woman is like a gun.

They are interesting and pretty to look at; however,

if you're not a wise person you might not want to invest in one.

A gun can be to your advantage or your disadvantage based on how you use them.

Guns come in all shapes and sizes, yet all of them can kill.

So can a woman.

If you expect a gun to perform properly, you have to keep up with its maintenance.

Same goes for a woman.

In order to keep a gun without a lot of hassles and troubles, you need a license.

So is the case of a woman.

Finally, if there ever comes a time when you need or want to dispose of a gun,

there are steps you have to follow to ensure everyone's safety.

Same goes for a woman.

Considering those things, I'm not ready to own a gun.

Nor am I ready to own a woman.

Friend in You

A long time ago, I once had a friend who I thought would
stick with me 'til the bitter end.

Come to find out, that just wasn't the case...

Never did I consider our friendship

would disappear before my very face.

Let me tell you about this shit...

and then see if you can relate to it.

He and I hung out a lot,

ripped up the town and occasionally

we'd both put up funds for some pot.

However, that's just the half.

Sometimes, we'd both crack dumb jokes 'til one of us
laughed.

Then other times we'd be kicking game to the broads or
just writing rhymes.

He had a special gift for singing a song...

Just give him a request and he could sing for you all
night long.

And if that wasn't enough for you; there were some other
things that he could do.

For instance he could cut hair, draw and repairs things
that need fixing.

I know 'cause I once watch him fix a device used for mixing.

Anyhow I told myself that eventually he would come into some wealth.

By him being my friend, I thought I'd make a little investment.

Not even noticing that at that point our friendship went.

All I'm trying to say is I wish our friendship hadn't gone that way.

But all things must come to an end, even if it is a good friend.

So when choosing friends just remember-

Just because they're here today don't mean they will be around in December.

My Father

My father is the only role model I've ever known.

When I was young, I wanted to be just like him even more now that I'm grown.

He always had me looking forward to something.

He even showed distinct class and grace for a man who had much of nothing.

My father showed me and my brothers and equal amount of love.

No wonder he's the greatest father I can think of!

He taught me how to be independent and strong.

And to trust in Jehovah for faith to carry on.

We even managed to have educational discussions and talks.

However, I liked it when he took us on our little walks.

Most fathers run out on their kids; however, my father never ever did.

He stuck with me and his problems 'til the bitter end…

My father (Norman Francis Williams) is my very best and special friend.

Determination Despite Obstacles

Before I head out the door, I say a short prayer-

To God and request that he sends an angel down here…

to journey with me through these dangerous streets.

I have to survive and all the while keep them
state issued boots off my feet.

People around me wilding out- especially the children.

Young mother giving birth then throwing their newborns
out of buildings.

And if that's not enough, the economy is going down and
prices are going up.

Our leader Mr. 666 and his "herd of beasts" are making it
impossible

for America and other nations to co-exist in peace.

Sometimes I feel like my life's all a set-up.

Still I can't let my emotions get fed up.

Satan has rendered victorious over a lot of lives,

but he'll never master mine.

'Cause when I look in the mirror the reflection of God
shines back,

plus, I'm a mastermind.

So I keep on keeping on…nothing can stop me.

If you drop me, I'll get up and come back for more unless
you pop me.

Tears Of A Primate

I represent man in his purest form-

so if you're lost just follow me and if you need to imitate

someone, model yourself after me.

Space yourself from bums and haters;

and if you catch the urge to sin,

think of the consequences you'll receive later.

Otherwise… the next time you walk out your door,

you might not come back home anymore.

Writer's Block

I have writer's block.

I can't think of anything worth writing about.

Still I have the duty as a poet to put some sort of poem out.

So I've decided to write a poem on my general thoughts about life for me as a whole.

1) Stay humble and in every situation know and play my role.
2) Don't make my life harder than what it has to be. Because no one has to live with the aftermath of my decisions except me.
3) I don't follow any one's path but my own. I never did it when I was young and I won't do it now that I'm grown.
4) Keep it real and always be upfront. Tell a person what they need to hear, not what they want.
5) I look in the mirror and I tell myself that I'm more than just an average human being. We all can't be gods and goddesses, but we all can be kings and queens.
6) Develop a sense of humor because I'm going to need it eventually; or else life's daily obstacles will get to me.

I could go on and on but as I said before…

I have writer's block---

So let me make this part of the poem be the place that I stop.

Shut Up Sometimes

A cellphone is the worst thing a woman can have.

If she had to choose who she would be loyal to between you and her phone,

our ass don't stand a chance.

Chicken heads cackling about nothing- wasting valuable airtime.

That's probably all that a broad can store within her mind.

A phone conversation about some guy she wants to fuck or another broad she can't stand;

She has the latest features on her cellphone plan;

however, after all that's said and done, she ain't got no man.

Alltel, Verizon, Nextel, and Sprint- she's never late on her phone bill, but she can't pay her rent.

Talk so much her minutes switched to roam…

Then she has the nerve to complain about the dysfunction within her home.

Learn to put that phone on silence and also your mouth-

Be a woman who's not afraid to confront her inner issues and work them out.

Cellphones were made with the idea of people having them for emergencies;

not for you to run your mouth on it talking constantly.

There's a multitude of females in this world who are all alone;

and they have only one thing to thank for that— their cellphones!

Precious Sun Of Mine

Elijah MacCoy Williams, son of mine.

Though I'm not with you every day, you constantly stay on my mind.

And that's something that hurts my heart.

To have a son whom I love, but we're so far apart.

However, in God's due time, he's going to bring us two closer together, & make everything just fine.

Listen to your mother & the rest of your elders, & make your daddy proud.

And know that things will get better for me & you, though it doesn't seem that way right now.

Bad times is only designed to make us stronger.

And God rewards his children who hold on & remain faithful longer.

So until we talk & see each other again, just know that you mean more to me than any family member or friend.

In my heart is where you are, & that's where you shall stay.

Your father loves you Elijah, for now & always.

Your Father Always,

Donald MacCoy Williams

We hope you enjoyed!

TEARS OF A PRIMATE

PRIMATE

Donald Williams was born and raised in Norfolk, Virginia. He still calls the magnificent city his home. After the birth of his son in 2012, Donald was determined to pen his first children's book just for his son.

Adrienne Cromer's Dedications:

My dedication is to the Lord God Almighty who is my most compassionate Father in Heaven.

Conscious of my weaknesses and of my many faults, I will always entrust myself to His loving care because I know that without Him I am nothing and would not be where I am today.

I thank and praise Him for loving me and my family and for His overall protection for us each day and night.

I will always acknowledge Him as my Everlasting Father who is over the heaven and the earth, who sustains me and who is always merciful to me.

John 3:16 For God so loved the world, that He gave His only begotten Son, that whosoever believeth in Him should not perish, but have everlasting life.

Adrienne M. Cromer

Tears Of A Primate